TO THEM OF THE LAST WAGON
and

WHO WAS THIS JESUS?

TO THEM OF THE LAST WAGON

and

WHO WAS THIS JESUS?

J. Reuben Clark Jr.

CLASSIC TALK SERIES

Deseret Book Company
Salt Lake City, Utah

Reprinted with permission.

Library of Congress Catalog Card Number: 97-078188

ISBN 0-87579-975-2

Printed in the United States of America

10   9   8   7   6   5   4   3   2   1   72082

TO THEM OF THE LAST
WAGON

My brethren and sisters, I should like in the beginning to add my testimony to the many that we have heard during this conference—my testimony that God lives, that Jesus is the Christ, the Redeemer of the world, the first fruits of the Resurrection; that Joseph Smith was a prophet; that through him the gospel was restored and likewise the priesthood, the authority delegated to man on earth to represent Deity here among us; and that the Prophet has been followed down to and including our present President, George Albert Smith, by men who possessed the keys of the last dispensation as conferred upon Joseph Smith.

The matter that I shall give you today is very dear to my soul. Since I should like to say what I have to say in the best way I can say it, I have written it down and shall read it. I hope that what I shall say will be in harmony with the spirit of this great conference, I think the greatest I have attended in its high spiritual tone.

At the near close of this one hundredth year of the entering into these valleys of your fathers and your mothers, some of yours and mine, I wish to speak a few further words of humble tribute and thanksgiving to them, and especially to the meekest and lowliest of them, those great souls, majestic in the simplicity of their faith and in their living testimony of the truth of the restored gospel, to those souls in name unknown, unremembered, unhonored in the pages of history, but lovingly revered round the hearthstones of their children and their children's children who pass down from generation to generation the story of their faith and their mighty works, and the righteousness of their lives and living, those souls who worked and worked, and prayed and followed, and wrought so gloriously.

I would not take away one word of praise or gratitude, honor or reverence from the great men who led these humble ones of ours. They were mighty men in brain and brawn, in courage and valor, in honesty and in love of truth, living near the Lord—Brothers Brigham and Heber and Wilford and Willard and Charles, the two Orsons and Parley, and John and George and Erastus and Lorenzo and Daniel and Joseph and Jedediah, and a host of other giants, each and all richly blessed with the Lord's divine love and with that gift of the Holy Ghost that made them leaders truly like unto

Moses of old. I yield, we yield, to no one in our
gratitude for them and for their work of direct-
ing the conquest of the wilderness and of saving
men's souls. Their names shine lustrously on
those pages of history which record only the
doings of the makers of epochs—those choice
spirits, chosen before the foundation of the
world, to be the leaders and builders of dispen-
sations of God's dealings with men; and these
leaders of ours to be the builders of that dispensation which of old was named the Dispensation
of the Fulness of Time. Unnumbered eternities
will remember and honor them.

But I should like now and here to say a few
words about those who trod after where those
giants led, some in the same companies that the
Brethren piloted, some in later companies following that year and the years after, some in the
fateful handcarts with their unexcelled devotion,
heroism, and faith, all trickling forward in a

never-failing, tiny stream, till they filled the valley they entered and then flowed out at the sides and ends, peopling this whole wilderness-waste which they fructified, making it to fulfil the ancient prophecy that the desert should blossom as the rose.

I would like to say something about the last wagon in each of the long wagon trains that toiled slowly over the plains, up mountain defiles, down steep, narrow canyons, and out into the valley floor that was to be home—this last wagon: last, because the ox team that pulled it was the smallest and leanest and weakest, and had the tenderest feet of any in the train, it was slow starting, and slow moving; last, because worn and creaking, it took more time to fix and to grease, for young Jimmy generally had trouble in getting the wagon jack under the "ex"; last, because its wind-rent cover was old and patched and took hours to mend and tie up

to keep out the storm; last, because the wife,
heavy with child, must rest till the very moment
of starting; last, because sickly little Bill, the last-
born, poorly nourished, must be washed and
coaxed to eat the rough food, all they had; last,
because with all his tasks—helping little Bill,
cooking and cleaning up the breakfast—Mother
was not able to help much—Father took a little
longer to yoke his cattle and to gird himself for
the day's labor; last, because his morning
prayers took a few more minutes than the others
spent—he had so many blessings to thank the
Lord for and some special blessings to ask the
Lord to grant, blessings of health and strength,
especially for his wife, and for little Bill, and for
the rest, and then the blessings for himself that
his own courage would not fail, but most of all
for the blessings of faith, faith in God and in the
Brethren who sometimes seemed so far away.
For they were out in front where the air was

clear and clean and where they had unbroken vision of the blue vault of heaven. The Brethren had really visioned the glory of the Lord, who walked near them, put his thoughts into their minds; his spirit guided and directed them, petitioned thereto by the thousands of Saints who were back in Winter Quarters, back in Iowa, back in the States, and beyond, even across the waters, for the faithful poured out their souls in fervent prayer to Almighty God that the Brethren should be inspired. The Saints buoyed up the Brethren out in front with encouragement, with praise, and sometimes even with adulation. Knowing the Brethren were prophets of God, the Saints gave them full confidence, daily, almost hourly, expressed. The Brethren lived in a world of commendation from friends and the tried and true Saints. Rarely was their word or their act questioned by the faithful

Saints. This was as it should be and had to be to
carry out the Lord's purposes.

But back in the last wagon, not always could
they see the Brethren way out in front, and the
blue heaven was often shut out from their sight
by heavy, dense clouds of the dust of the earth.
Yet day after day, they of the last wagon pressed
forward, worn and tired, footsore, sometimes
almost disheartened, borne up by their faith that
God loved them, that the restored gospel was
true, and that the Lord led and directed the
Brethren out in front. Sometimes, they in the last
wagon glimpsed, for an instant, when faith
surged strongest, the glories of a celestial world,
but it seemed so far away, and the vision so
quickly vanished because want and weariness
and heartache and sometimes discouragement
were always pressing so near. When the vision
faded, their hearts sank. But they prayed again
and pushed on, with little praise, with not too

much encouragement, and never with adulation. For there was nearly always something wrong with the last wagon or with its team—the off ox was a little lame in the right front shoulder; the hub of the left front wheel was often hot; the tire of the hind wheel on the same side was loose. So corrective counsel, sometimes strong reproof, was the rule, because the wagon must not delay the whole train. But yet in that last wagon there was devotion and loyalty and integrity, and above and beyond everything else, faith in the Brethren and in God's power and goodness. For had not the Lord said that "not even a sparrow falleth unnoticed by the Father, and were they not of more value than sparrows?" And then they had their testimony burning always like an eternal fire on a holy altar, that the restored gospel was true, and that Joseph was a prophet of God, and that Brigham was Joseph's chosen successor.

When the train moved forward in the early morning sun and the oxen with a swinging pull that almost broke the tongue got the last wagon on the move, the dust in the still morning air hung heavy over the road. Each wagon from the first stirred up its own cloud, till when the last wagon swung into line, that dust was dense and suffocating. It covered the last wagon and all that was in it; it clung to clothes; it blackened faces; it filled eyes already sore, and ears. The wife, soon to be a mother, could hardly catch her breath in the heavy, choking dust, for even in the pure air she breathed hard from her burden. Each jolt of the wagon, for those ahead had made wagon ruts almost "ex" deep, wrung from her clenched lips a half-groan she did her best to keep from the ears of the anxious, solicitous husband plodding slowly along, guiding and goading the poor dumb cattle, themselves weary from the long trek. So through the long day of jolting and discomfort and sometimes pain, sometimes panting for breath, the mother, anxious only that the unborn babe should not be injured, rode, for she could not walk; and the children walked, for the load was too heavy and big for them to ride; and the father walked sturdily alongside and prayed.

When in the evening the last wagon creaked slowly into its place in the circle corral, and the Brethren came to inquire how the day had gone with the mother, then joy leaped in their hearts, for had not the Brethren remembered them? New hope was born, weariness fled, fresh will to do was enkindled; gratitude to God was poured out for their knowledge of the truth, for their testimony that God lived, that Jesus was the Christ, that Joseph was a prophet, that Brigham was his ordained successor, and that for the righteous a crown of glory awaited that should be theirs during the eternities of the life to come.

Then they would join in the songs and dancing in the camp, making the camp's gaiety their own, as much as Mother's condition would permit.

Then the morning came when from out that last wagon floated the la-la of the newborn babe, and mother love made a shrine, and Father bowed in reverence before it. But the train must move on. So out into the dust and dirt the last wagon moved again, swaying and jolting, while Mother eased as best she could each pain-giving jolt so no harm might be done her, that she might be strong to feed the little one, bone of her bone, flesh of her flesh. Who will dare to say that angels did not cluster round and guard her and ease her rude bed, for she had given another choice spirit its mortal body that it might work out its God-given destiny?

My mother was one of those babes so born in 1848, ninety-nine years ago.

Another morning came, when courageous little Bill, who, with a hero's heart, had trudged through long days of hot sun and through miles of soggy mud in the rain, his little body drenched, little Bill, weak and wan, must be crowded in to ride with Mother, for he was sick from a heavy cold. Months before, on that cold winter's night when they fled Nauvoo for their lives to escape the fiendish wrath of a wild mob, Bill became dangerously ill with pneumonia, which left him with weak lungs. This old illness now returned. He grew worse and worse. The elders came and prayed he might get well. But the Lord wanted little Bill with him. So a few mornings later a weeping mother and a grief-stricken father and that last wagon swung into place in the line, leaving beside the road, under some scrub brush a little mound, unmarked save for heaped-up rocks to keep out the wolves, a mound that covered another martyr to the cause of truth.

So through dust and dirt, dirt and dust, during the long hours, the longer days—that grew into weeks and then into months, they crept along till, passing down through its portals, the valley welcomed them to rest and home. The cattle dropped to their sides, wearied almost to death; nor moved they without goading, for they too sensed they had come to the journey's end.

That evening was the last of the great trek, the mightiest trek that history records since Israel's flight from Egypt, and as the sun sank below the mountain peaks of the west and the eastern crags were bathed in an amethyst glow that was a living light, while the western mountainsides were clothed in shadows of the rich blue of the deep sea, they of the last wagon, and of the wagon before them, and of the one before that, and so to the very front wagon of the train, these all sank to their knees in the joy of their souls, thanking God that at last they were in Zion. "Zion, Zion, lovely Zion; Beautiful Zion; Zion, city of our God!" They knew there was a God, for only he could have brought them, triumphant, militant, through all the scorn, the ridicule, the slander, the tarrings and featherings, the whippings, the burnings, the plunderings, the murderings, the ravishings of wives and daughters, that had been their lot, the lot of their people since Joseph visioned the Father and the Son.

But hundreds of these stalwart souls of undoubting faith and great prowess, were not yet at their journey's end.

Brother Brigham again called them to the colors of the kingdom of God, and sent them to settle the valleys, near and remote, in these vast mountains of refuge. So again they yoked their oxen and hitched up their teams, and putting their all in the covered wagon, this time willingly, unwhipped by the threat of mob cruelty and outrage, they wended their slow way to new valleys, again trusting with implicit faith in the wisdom and divine guidance of their Moses. The very elements obeyed their faith, faith close kin to that which made the world.

These tens of thousands who so moved and so built were the warp and the woof of Brother Brigham's great commonwealth. Without them Brother Brigham had failed his mission. These were the instruments—the shovelers, the plowers, and the sowers and reapers, the machinists, the architects, the masons, the woodworkers, the organ builders, the artisans, the mathematicians, the men of letters, all gathered from the four corners of the earth, furnished by the Lord to Brother Brigham and the prophet leaders who came after, that he and they might direct the working out of His purposes. These wrought as God inspired Brother Brigham and the other prophets to plan, all to the glory of God and the up-building of his kingdom.

Upright men they were, and fearless, unmindful of what men thought or said of them, if they were in their line of duty. Calumny, slander, derision, scorn left them unmoved, if they were treading the straight and narrow way. Uncaring they were of men's blame and censure, if the Lord approved them. Unswayed they were by the praise of men, to wander from the path of truth. Endowed by the spirit of discernment, they knew when kind words were mere courtesy, and when they betokened honest interest. They moved neither to the right nor to the left from the path of truth to court the good favor of men.

So for a full hundred years, urged by the spirit of gathering and led by a burning testimony

of the truth of the restored gospel, thousands
upon tens of thousands of these humble souls,
one from a city, two from a family, have bidden
farewell to friends and homes and loved ones,
and with sundered heartstrings, companioned
with privation and with sacrifice even to life
itself, these multitudes have made their way to
Zion, to join those who were privileged to come
earlier, that all might build up the kingdom of
God on earth—all welded together by common
hardship and suffering, never-ending work and
deep privation, tragic woes and heart-eating
griefs, abiding faith and exalting joy, firm testimony and living spiritual knowledge—a mighty
people, missioned with the salvation, not only of
the living, but of the dead also, saviors not wor-
shipers of their ancestors, their hearts aglow with
the divine fire of the spirit of Elijah, who turns
the hearts of the fathers to the children and of the
children to the fathers.

And thousands upon thousands of these tens of thousands, from the first till now, all the elect of God, measured to their humble calling and to their destiny as fully as Brother Brigham and the others measured to theirs, and God will so reward them. They were pioneers in word and thought and act and faith, even as were they of more exalted station. The building of this inter-mountain empire was not done in a corner by a select few but by this vast multitude flowing in from many nations, who came and labored and wrought, faithfully following their divinely called leaders.

In living our lives let us never forget that the deeds of our fathers and mothers are theirs, not ours; that their works cannot be counted to our glory; that we can claim no excellence and no place because of what they did; that we must rise by our own labor, and that labor failing we shall fail. We may claim no honor, no reward, no respect, nor special position or recognition, no credit because of what our fathers were or what they wrought. We stand upon our own feet in our own shoes. There is no aristocracy of birth in this Church; it belongs equally to the highest and the lowliest; for as Peter said to Cornelius, the Roman centurion, seeking him: "Of a truth I perceive that God is no respecter of persons: But in every nation he that feareth him, and worketh righteousness, is accepted with him" (Acts 10:34–35).

So to these humble but great souls, our fathers and mothers, the tools of the Lord, who have, for this great people, hewed the stones and laid the foundations of God's Kingdom, solid as the granite mountains from which they carved the rocks for their temple, to these humble souls, great in faith, great in work, great in righteous living, great in fashioning our priceless heritage, I humbly render my love, my respect, my reverent homage. God keep their memories ever fresh among us, their children, to help us meet our duties even as they met theirs, that God's work may grow and prosper till the restored gospel of Jesus Christ rules all nations and all peoples, till peace, Christ's peace, shall fill the whole earth, till "righteousness shall cover the earth even as the waters cover the mighty deep." Let us here and now dedicate all that we have and all that we are to this divine work. May God help us so to do, I humbly pray in Jesus' name, his Son, amen.

This talk was originally delivered in the Sunday afternoon session of general conference, 5 October 1947, while President Clark was serving as first counselor in the First Presidency.

WHO WAS THIS JESUS?

My brothers and sisters: It is a very humbling experience to stand before a great audience of students who are seeking truth. I humbly pray that you will help me with your faith and prayers that I may say something that will be helpful to all of us.

President Jensen observed that this building had not quite the atmosphere of the Joseph Smith Building. I agree. But one of the most inspirational meetings that I have ever attended was held down in a coal mine, where there was no adornment, little physical light, but an abundance of the inner light upon which we must ultimately depend in our journey through life.

At the end of the great vision which God gave to Moses on the Mount, recorded in the first chapter of Moses, God said to Moses: "For behold, this is my work and my glory—to bring to pass the immortality and eternal life of man" (Moses 1:39).

In that great intercessory prayer which the Savior offered up after they had left the upper chamber, on the way to Gethsemane, he voiced this basic truth: "And this is life eternal, that they might know thee the only true God, and Jesus Christ, whom thou hast sent" (John 17:3).

To know the Christ is the duty of all of us, and not alone our duty, but our privilege; and to know him is eternal life, the life which we all seek.

As I contemplated what I might say to you

today, it occurred to me that perhaps if I were to begin with the question, "Who was this Jesus, who is the Christ?" and then give some suggestive considerations in answer, it might be useful.

I sometimes wonder whether our concept of the Christ is not somewhat circumscribed within the limits of his mortal service. We think of him as the lowly Carpenter, living in a lowly home, going through his life mission, befriended sometimes, scoffed and scorned at other times, and finally, crucified by his own. We read of his miracles, we read of his great teachings, the great truths which he gave to us, but we think of him very largely as a mortal being. Some may judge his Messiahship by his mortal service. This service, properly understood, will give the true picture; but too often there is incomplete understanding.

We might begin by recalling that Christ is the First Born of the Father; the Only Begotten of the

Father (and we add according to the flesh). He sits on the right hand of the Father. He acts for and in behalf of the Father, as an agent of the Father "to reign with almighty power according to the will of the Father" (D&C 20:24).

As bearing upon his personality, I thought perhaps this morning, if I were to read you a little scripture and make a few comments thereon, it might help us to get a little better view of Christ than we might now have. I am going to read from Moses, first chapter, the 31st verse and following, and then I want to make a few observations thereon.

THE LORD'S STATEMENT ABOUT HIS CREATIVES

God had shown Moses this earth and the inhabitants thereof. Satan then came and tempted Moses, but Moses resisted and rebuked him. Calling upon the Lord, Moses heard a voice that came from heaven and a great vision of the earth and its inhabitants was opened to him. So mighty was the vision that—

> . . . the glory of the Lord was upon Moses, so that Moses stood in the presence of God, and talked with him face to face. And the Lord God said unto Moses: For mine own purpose have I made these things. Here is wisdom and it remaineth in me.
>
> And by the word of my power, have I created them, which is mine Only Begotten Son, who is full of grace and truth.
>
> AND WORLDS WITHOUT NUMBER HAVE I CREATED: and I also created them for mine own purpose; and BY THE SON I CREATED THEM, WHICH IS MINE ONLY BEGOTTEN.
>
> And the first man of all men have I called Adam, which is many.
>
> BUT ONLY AN ACCOUNT OF THIS EARTH, and the inhabitants thereof, GIVE I UNTO YOU. FOR BEHOLD, THERE ARE MANY WORLDS THAT HAVE PASSED AWAY BY THE WORD OF MY POWER. AND THERE ARE MANY THAT NOW STAND, AND INNUMERABLE ARE THEY

UNTO MAN; but all things are numbered
unto me, for they are mine and I know them.

And it came to pass that Moses spake unto
the Lord, saying: Be merciful unto thy servant, O God, and tell me concerning this
earth, and the inhabitants thereof, and also
the heavens, and then thy servant will be con-
tent.

And the Lord God spake unto Moses, saying: THE HEAVENS, THEY ARE MANY,
AND THEY CANNOT BE NUMBERED
UNTO MAN: but they are numbered unto
me, for they are mine.

And as one earth shall pass away, and the
heavens thereof even so shall another come;
and there is no end to my works, neither to
my words (emphasis added).

THE ASTRONOMERS' UNIVERSE

I am somewhat interested in popular articles
dealing with astronomy. I am not an astronomer;
I have never studied astronomy; I am not going
to try to give you an astronomical lecture; but I
do want to call your attention to two or three

statements by astronomers that give point to these words of Moses' vision, "worlds without number . . . innumerable . . . unto man . . . The heavens, they are many, and they cannot be numbered unto man."

All these were created by God, through the agency and the instrumentality of Jesus Christ, the Only Begotten of the Father, to know whom, along with God, is eternal life. What I shall recite to you about the universe is what astronomers have said in the last several months.

Recently—within the last two or three years—two great telescopes have been set up, one a 200-inch telescope and the other a 48-inch, the first known as the Hale instrument, and the other as the Schmidt. These are located at Mount Palomar, California.

The 200-inch telescope reaches farther out into space than man has ever reached before. I may say here that the astronomical measuring rod of space is the light year, that is, the distance light will travel, traveling 186,000 miles per second, in one year. This Hale instrument, the 200-incher, as they sometimes call it, reaches out into space to the distance of a billion light years—a billion light years.

That instrument, together with the Schmidt instrument, has enabled the astronomers to estimate that, within the radius of a billion light years, there are one hundred millions of "tremendous formations of stars, dust, and gas, called nebulae, or galaxies," each more or less the counterpart of our own great galaxy, the Milky Way; our only claim to distinction being that "our own galaxy . . . is about as big as they come." One hundred millions of galaxies within our present visual radius, and who can guess how many beyond! Indeed, "innumerable" are the works of God to man.

As our own galaxy has its own, indeed is its

own heaven, so must it be with other galaxies; neither can the heavens be now numbered by man, even as God told Moses. There is opinion that these galaxies are distributed through space uniformly.

OUR MILKY WAY GALAXY

Just a few words about our own Milky Way galaxy: It is supposed to contain a hundred billion stars. Another astronomer speaks of five billion, and another of a billion. Whether any or all of these stars have planetary systems associated with them such as our sun has, we do not know, scientifically. The astronomers say there could be stored "a million times as many stars in the present volume of the system without the risk of an undue frequency of stellar collisions."

This galaxy of ours is said to be about a hundred thousand light years in diameter. (Another figure I have seen is 200,000 light years.) The astronomers say our galaxy is in the shape of a disc or wheel, which is about 20,000 light years thick. It is slowly revolving about a group of stars that seem to be the hub. These are not visible to us so far. They are supposed to lie in the constellation Sagittarius, which is low down on our southern horizon and can be seen in the months of June and July, beginning in May and ending in August. Incidentally, what they call "cosmic static" is coming from that great center. This static also emanates from other portions of the Milky Way.

As I say, the stars of our galaxy are revolving like a great wheel around a hub of stars. It takes 200 million years for our solar system to make one revolution, the system traveling at the rate of 150 miles per second. We are out towards the outer edge of this great disc or wheel, perhaps 30,000 light years from the hub. We lie near the center plane of the disc. There is a cloud of cosmic dust between us and the hub, which cuts off our view of it. Our system is floating in a cloud of cosmic haze. Some say that our galaxy has "outward-spiraling pinwheel arms" in which a large part of our billion or billions of stars are located. Our solar system may be in one of these areas.

REGARDING THE HUB OF OUR GALAXY

In reference to this hub group of stars around which the other units of the galaxy revolve, we might well recall what God said to Abraham at the beginning of the mighty vision he had, in which God outlined the history of the creation of the earth on which we stand. Abraham records:

> And I saw the stars, that they were very great, and that one of them was nearest unto the throne of God; and there were many great ones which were near unto it;
>
> And the Lord said unto me: These are the governing ones; and the name of the great one is Kolob, because it is near unto me, for I am the Lord thy God: I have set this one to

govern all those which belong to the same order as that upon which thou standest (Abraham 3:2–3).

With all these great creations in mind, let us now recall the words of God (already quoted) to Moses:

> And by the word of my power, have I created them, which is mine Only Begotten Son, who is full of grace and truth.
>
> And worlds without number have I created; and I also created them for mine own purpose; and by the Son I created them, which is mine Only Begotten.
>
> . . . For behold, there are many worlds that have passed away by the word of my power . . . and innumerable are they unto man;
>
> . . . The heavens, they are many, and they cannot be numbered unto man; but they are numbered unto me, for they are mine (Moses 1:32–37).

In Abraham's record of his great vision, he tells us the Lord said to him:

My son, my son (and his hand was stretched out), behold I will show you all these. And he put his hand upon mine eyes, and I saw those things which his hands had made, which were many; and they multiplied before mine eyes, and I could not see the end thereof (Abraham 3:12).

How gloriously the Psalmist sang:

When I consider thy heavens, the work of thy fingers, the moon and the stars, which thou hast ordained;

What is man, that thou art mindful of him? and the son of man, that thou visitest him? (Psalm 8:4).

This World-Maker, this Maker of Universes, and their destroyer, he it was who came to this earth; he is the lowly Jesus; born in an inn, wrapped in swaddling clothes; cradled in a manger.

Behold him in his role—the Creator and Destroyer of Universes, as the Agent of God, then how very simple and commonplace seem the miracles which he performed and which are giving so much trouble to our rationalists.

SOME MIRACLES OF JESUS

I have thought of some of those miracles in the sense of their being the miracle of a creator, demonstrating his creative power, particularly some that I call creative miracles: the turning of water into wine, how simple that must have been to a deity who made universes; the feeding of the 5,000, how simple that was.

And I hope none of you students will be disturbed by this pygmy-rationalizing which suggests that the multitude was fed on lunches which they brought with them. This Creator of the Universe, out of five loaves and two fishes, made food that fed them all. Perhaps, in order to silence the criticism which might be made, or the explanation, that he just hypnotized them and they were all just hypnotized, the record says, "And they took up twelve baskets full of the fragments" (Mark 6:43). Of equal importance and stature was the feeding of the 4,000 at a later time (see Matthew 15:37).

Other miracles prove he had control of the elements. I am thinking of the night when he was sleeping in the prow of the boat and a great storm arose. The Apostles were terrified. They awakened him. He calmed the storm. And after this feeding of the 5,000, when he journeyed across the water, walking upon it, I recall how frightened were the Apostles in the boat, thinking he was a spirit.

You can almost hear him call to them: "It is I; be not afraid" (Matthew 14:27). Peter asked, "Bid me come unto thee on the water." Jesus answered: "Come." Peter stepped out upon the water and started to walk, but his heart and his faith failed him at the sight of the boisterous waves. He started to sink. Jesus stretched forth his hand and saved him, reproving him thus:

"O thou of little faith, wherefore didst thou doubt?" (Matthew 14:28–31).

Jesus had control of the animal kingdom. You remember the miraculous draft of fishes, when he first called Peter and James and John. They had been out fishing all night, but had caught nothing. He asked to get into their boat that he might speak to the multitude; he shoved out from the shore, so that the multitude could not press too much around him.

When he finished speaking he said, "Launch out into the deep, and let down your nets for a draught." They replied they had been fishing all night, and had caught nothing. Nevertheless, at his word they cast their net and it was filled with fish, so much so that the net brake and they had to call for James and John to come out in another boat. Peter, the great Peter, bowed before the Savior. "Depart from me," he said, "for I am a sinful man" (Matthew 5:4–8).

And later, a similar experience, on the shores of the same Galilee, after the resurrection, when Peter and the rest had gone fishing, not under-standing there was work in the Lord's service for them to do. They had fished all night and caught nothing. In the early light of the morning they saw a man on the shore; there was a little fire. A voice came from the shore: "Cast the net on the right side of the ship, and ye shall find." They did, and it was filled. John, perhaps recol-lecting the early experience, said, "It is the Lord." Peter, wrapping his cloak about him, for he was naked (he did not want to appear before the Lord nude), cast himself into the sea and waded to the shore. And there they ate, appar-ently the Savior eating with them. It was there that Peter got his command, "Feed my sheep" (see John 21:6–17).

The lowly Jesus thus had control of the animal life.

Finally, the vegetable kingdom came under his domination, also, for he cursed the barren fig tree as he went by. Some scholars have a great deal of difficulty in understanding that miracle. It looks rather simple to me, maybe too simple. But I get from this miracle the principle that he who does not do the things which his Creator fitted him to do, stands in danger of a reprimand. You cannot be barren with the intelligence, the talents, which God has given to you.

How great to mortals are these and the other miracles of Jesus, but how incomparably simple to the maker and destroyer of universes. Shall we further doubt the power of Jesus to do the service he performed on earth?

THE COUNCIL IN HEAVEN

But I wish to return for a few further observations upon Christ's divine agency for the Father, and a specific use he made of it in creating a world.

You will remember the Great Council of Heaven, of which the Lord told Abraham in the great vision, parts of the record of which we have already quoted. You will find the record in the Book of Abraham, and I would like all of you young people to read it. After recounting the meeting of the Father in the Great Council of Heaven, with the intelligences among whom he dwelt, and after telling that among these intelligences were those whom he would make his rulers, Abraham being one, the record continues:

> And there stood one among them that was like unto God, and he said unto those who were with him: We will go down, for there is space there, and we will take of these materials, and we will make an earth whereon these may dwell (Abraham 3:24).

You will kindly note two things in this statement: First, "There is space there." The Maker of Worlds knew where there was space in the universe. In the next place, the earth was to be made out of materials in space. This passage, given more than a hundred years ago, contradicts that theological idea of the time that the world was made out of nothing.

Our astronomers tell us today that so far as they can judge, the universes, those hundred millions of them, were made from star dust and gas that float about in great clouds in the interstellar spaces. Our own galaxy still has these great clouds of gas floating around, out of which, perhaps, in the due time of the Lord, other systems will be created. As already stated, we ourselves, are floating in a cosmic haze of dust.

THE CREATION OF THE EARTH

In this Council of Heaven, the purpose of creating the earth was unfolded to these assembled intelligences. The record then states, after noting the rebellion in heaven of Satan and his followers:

And then the Lord said: Let us go down.

And they went down at the beginning, and
they, that is the Gods, organized and formed
the heavens and the earth (Abraham 4:1).

The earth was made in order that the intelligences among whom God came down in this
great Council, might come to this earth and
"prove themselves" whether they would keep
the commandments of the Lord.

Only those who kept their first estate were to
come to this earth. That we are here proves that
we kept our first estate. If we keep this, our second estate, we shall have "glory added upon
[our] heads for ever and ever." We keep our second estate by doing whatsoever the Lord
commands us to do (see Abraham 3:25–26).

To the Only Begotten was committed the task
of creating the earth and all that it contains. John
declared: "All things were made by him; and
without him was not any thing made that was
made" (John 1:3).

THE FALL

Well, you know the story: First came Adam, and when the world was ready, Eve was given to Adam. The Lord said to Adam:

> And I, the Lord God, commanded the man, saying: Of every tree of the garden thou mayest freely eat.
>
> But of the tree of the knowledge of good and evil, thou shalt not eat of it, nevertheless, thou mayest choose for thyself, for it is given unto thee; but, remember that I forbid it, for in the day thou eatest thereof thou shalt surely die (Moses 3:16–17).

Eve ate. Adam ate. This was the Fall. I have never considered the Fall as a real sin, because when the situation was explained to Adam and to Eve, Adam rejoiced at what had happened, and Eve said, "Were it not for our transgression we never should have had seed" (Moses 5:11). This meant that if Adam and Eve had remained in the Garden in their primal state, we should not have been born, and we should have had no mortal bodies, and the purpose of the plan evolved in the Great Council in Heaven would have come to naught.

The Fall of Adam brought two deaths into the world. Before the Fall, Adam and Eve walked and talked with God in the Garden. The Fall took them away from the presence of God. That was a spiritual death and comes to be known in our scriptures as the second death.

The other death was the mortal death. Our bodies die and go back to mother earth from which they came. Unless we had been redeemed from this mortal death, we could not have been reunited with our spirits, and the great plan of the Creator would have been defeated, which plan is based upon the fact, as we all know, that we lived before we came here, that we live here, tabernacled in the flesh, and that after our death, which separates spirit and body, and our body goes to the grave, there is, under the eternal plan, a re-uniting of the body and of the spirit, making the perfect soul, a re-uniting which gives us the power to fulfill the destiny that is ours, of eternal progression.

THE ATONEMENT

It was necessary, therefore, that something should be done in order to make it possible for body and spirit to be reunited.

Moses records that it was revealed to Adam that the Only Begotten was to come to earth and offer himself as a sacrifice to satisfy the demands of the Fall. So, in due time, the Only Begotten did come; he was born; not in a palace, not as a direct descendant of an immediate king, though royal blood was in his mortal veins, but he was born in an inn, wrapped in swaddling clothes, cradled in a manger. Angels heralded his birth. Those who knew, came to worship.

The Prophets from Adam down, spoke of him

and his coming. Enoch was fully instructed, indeed, had a vision of the crucifixion. Noah was likewise instructed. Jesus himself used the scriptures to show he was the Christ, both to the two disciples on the way to Emmaus when the Lord began his explanation by referring to Moses, and in the evening when he appeared to the Apostles, ten of them in the Upper Chamber.

The Psalms spoke of him, several of them, but particularly Psalms 2, 8, 16, 22; Psalm 22 being a beautifully poetic description of the horrors of a crucifixion. Isaiah predicted his coming, and declared names by which he should be called. The wise men quoted scripture declaring the place of Christ's birth.

On this hemisphere, from the earliest history of the Nephites, the name of the Savior was declared, where he was to be born, the name of his mother, and the purpose and effect of his taking on mortality fully explained.

Jesus came and lived his life through. Then he gave it, "no man took it from him," in order that you and I and all mankind might have the ability to regain our spirits and become immortal. This redeemed us from the mortal death brought by the Fall. This salvation is granted to every soul born to this earth.

The other death, the spiritual death, we, ourselves, must overcome. It is for us, ourselves, to gain our way back into the presence of God, and we do it by knowing Christ, and knowing him, then by keeping his commandments.

What a glorious plan it was, and is, and how glorious is the Man, the God, who, as the agent of the Father, brought this about. For God he is, as John in that great symphony of thought which opens his Gospel, declares: "In the beginning was the Word, and the Word was with God, and the Word was God."

God grant that this testimony, this knowledge

of the Christ, may come to all of us. God give unto us some, and at least partially adequate, understanding of the Christ, and who he is, and what his work was and is, and what he did for us, and of our everlasting debt to him, to the end that we may rejoice in him, give honor to him, and through him gain eternal life.

God grant this.

I bear my testimony that Jesus was this Christ, this World Maker, this builder and destroyer of universes, that he died for the sins of the world, that is, to redeem us and each of us from the mortal death brought by the Fall, and that to know him is eternal life.

God give to all of us a knowledge of these great and basic truths, I humbly pray, in the name of Jesus, the Only Begotten Son, amen.

From an address given to the Brigham Young University student body on 11 December 1951, when President Clark was serving as second counselor in the First Presidency.